AUSTRALIA

REESE EVERETT

Rourke
Educational Media

rourkeeducationalmedia.com

FEB 2019

Before Reading:

Building Academic Vocabulary and Background Knowledge

Before reading a book, it is important to tap into what your child or students already know about the topic. This will help them develop their vocabulary, increase their reading comprehension, and make connections across the curriculum.

1. Look at the cover of the book. What will this book be about?
2. What do you already know about the topic?
3. Let's study the Table of Contents. What will you learn about in the book's chapters?
4. What would you like to learn about this topic? Do you think you might learn about it from this book? Why or why not?
5. Use a reading journal to write about your knowledge of this topic. Record what you already know about the topic and what you hope to learn about the topic.
6. Read the book.
7. In your reading journal, record what you learned about the topic and your response to the book.
8. After reading the book complete the activities below.

Content Area Vocabulary
Read the list. What do these words mean?

colonizers

federal

immigration

indigenous

lingo

monolith

penal

staple

teems

vast

After Reading:

Comprehension and Extension Activity

After reading the book, work on the following questions with your child or students in order to check their level of reading comprehension and content mastery.

1. Why is Australia's wildlife unique? (Summarize)
2. What events in the past still affect the lives of Aboriginal people? (Infer)
3. When is summertime in Australia? (Asking Questions)
4. What did you read in the book that surprised you about the Australian continent? (Text to Self Connection)
5. Why is Australia's population so diverse? (Asking Questions)

Extension Activity

Explore the Outback! Research the terrain, the animals, and the dangers. Create a character, develop a plot, and write a story set in the Outback using realistic details from your research.

Table of Contents

States In Australia:
- New South Wales
- Queensland
- South Australia
- Tasmania
- Victoria
- Western Australia

The Land Down Under

Welcome to Oz! Some call Australia "the land down under" because of its location in the Southern Hemisphere. Australia is the smallest, lowest, and flattest of Earth's seven continents, with a land area of about 2.97 million square miles (7.69 million square kilometers). Aside from Antarctica, it is also the driest.

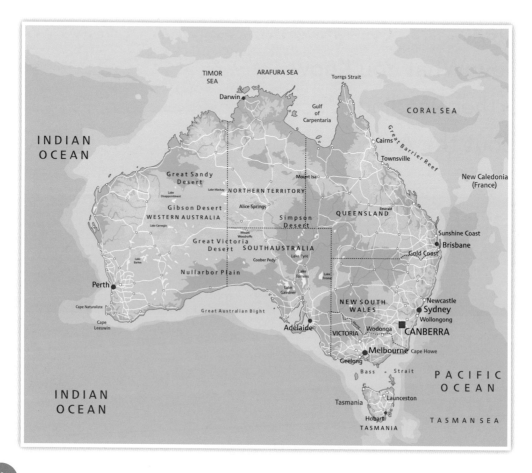

South Australian vineyard

Mount Hotham, Australia

Ventnor beach on Phillip Island, off the southern coast of Australia

It is summertime in Australia from December to February. March to May is fall. Winter occurs from June to August, and spring from September to November. May to October is the dry season, with clear, sunny skies. December to March is the wet season, with hot, humid weather and daily rainstorms.

Deserts cover about 18 percent of the continent. But there are also tropical rainforests and snowcapped mountains! Mount Kosciuszko is Australia's highest mountain. It rises 7,310 feet (2,228 meters) above sea level.

Mount Kosciuszko is the main range of the Snowy Mountains in Kosciuszko National Park.

Elabana Falls In Lamington National Park is one of the most-photographed waterfalls on Earth. Lamington is part of the Gondwana Rainforests of Australia World Heritage Area.

The Gondwana Rainforests of Australia are the most extensive area of subtropical rainforest in the world.

Unlike most continents, Australia only has one country: Australia! The Commonwealth of Australia, to be exact. Australia became an independent nation January 1, 1901. The country is both a representative democracy and a constitutional monarchy.

The Australian Constitution defines how the Commonwealth operates. The Australian Parliament is the **federal** government. It includes the Queen, represented by the Governor-General, the Senate, and the House of Representatives.

Parliament members meet at Parliament House in Australia's capital city, Canberra. The building is a symbol of Australia's democracy.

Australia has six states: New South Wales, Queensland, South Australia, Tasmania, Victoria, and Western Australia. Each has its own constitution. Power is shared between the federal government and individual states.

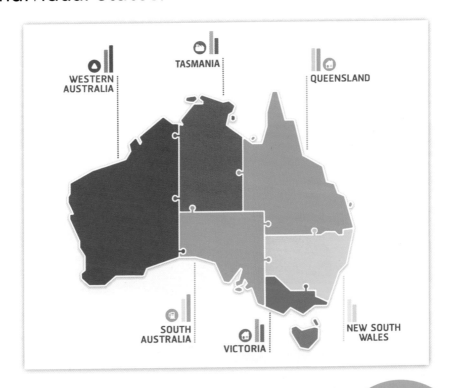

Australia is one of the wealthiest Asia–Pacific nations. Some of its major industries include finance, manufacturing, information and technology, agriculture, mining, and telecommunication.

Wild Australia

Australia **teems** with unique wildlife. This is because it has been isolated for millions of years, since it broke off from the supercontinent Gondwana. Nearly 90 percent of Australia's reptiles, 87 percent of its mammals, and 45 percent of its birds are endemic. This means they aren't found anywhere else on Earth.

kookaburra

gang-gang cockatoo

rainbow lorikeets

bearded dragon

frilled lizard

perentie

Australia is one of 17 countries identified as "mega-diverse." It has more mammals, birds, reptiles, and amphibians than 95 percent of the world's nations. There are 700 species of lizards alone!

Australia is famous for its kangaroos. But dingoes, wallabies, platypuses, emus, echidnas, and wombats all call the continent home.

kangaroo

dingo

platypus

The Outback is a 2.5 million mile (6.5 million square kilometer) dry, remote region of Australia. Only about 60 thousand people live in the Outback, mostly in small villages. But the **vast** area is home to many plants and animals, including budgerigars, cockatoos, dingoes, and wild horses called brumbies.

red-necked wallaby

wombat

emu

echidna

Australia is also famous for its dangerous animals, including 17 species of the world's most venomous snakes. The eastern brown snake is found all over Australia. It is likely to blame for most snakebite deaths.

eastern brown snake

The continent's other deadly wildlife includes saltwater crocodiles—and honey bees! The little buzzers kill more people on average than sharks or spiders.

saltwater crocodile

honey bee

The cassowary, found in Australia's rainforests, is classified as the world's most dangerous bird.

The Great Barrier Reef, off the coast of Queensland, is Earth's largest collection of coral reefs. Stretching more than 1,430 miles (2,300 kilometers), it is the largest living structure on the planet.

Its beauty and wildlife abundance make the reef a popular tourist destination. More than 100 jellyfish species, 133 types of sharks and rays, 1,625 types of fish, and 600 types of soft and hard corals are found there.

The most venomous marine animal in the world is found in the waters of the Great Barrier Reef. The sting of an Australian box jellyfish is often fatal.

People and Culture

The first Australians to inhabit the continent were the Aboriginals and Torres Strait Islanders. Researchers think they arrived in Australia 65,000 years ago. At one time, there were more than 500 clans and hundreds of distinct Aboriginal languages. For thousands of years, these **indigenous** people had Australia to themselves. When **colonizers** arrived, new diseases, oppressive land policies, and racism devastated the indigenous people.

Captain James Cook (1728 – 1779) claimed Australia as a British territory in 1770. In 1788, British ships carrying troops, women, children, and more than 700 convicts arrived to establish a **penal** colony called New South Wales. About 160,000 convicted criminals were sent to Australia to serve their sentences over the next 80 years.

Before British colonization, there were an estimated 750 thousand indigenous people on the continent. Australia's population now includes nearly 25 million people. About 20 percent of them are descendants of British convicts. Indigenous people make up less than three percent of Australia's current population.

More than half of Aboriginal people now live in towns or on the outskirts, sometimes in awful conditions. Some work as laborers on cattle ranches. Others maintain traditional lifestyles as hunters and gatherers.

Aboriginal people often live in poverty. They still struggle for land rights and equality. The Australian government has taken steps to make things better, but there is more to be done.

May 26 was established as National Sorry Day in 1998 to apologize for a government policy that took Aboriginal children from their families between 1910 and the 1970s. It was later renamed the National Day of Healing.

Because of its high levels of **immigration**, modern Australia has one of the world's most diverse populations, with a variety of races, cultures, and languages. Australians identify with more than 270 ancestries and speak more than 200 languages. About 26 percent of residents were born in another country. The rich cultural diversity is considered central to Australia's national identity.

Flinders Street Station is an iconic meeting place in Melbourne, Australia. The railway station is used by more than 100 thousand commuters daily. If someone tells you "Meet me under the clocks," this is where you go!

There is no official language in Australia, but English is spoken by most everyone. Aussie English is peppered with unique **lingo** called *strine* or *Ozspeak*. The word strine comes from "Aus-strine," which is how Aussies say Australian. Here's some translated strine:

Arvo: Afternoon
Bloke: Man
Bonnet: Hood of a car
Boot: Trunk of a car
Give it a burl: Try it
Have a yarn: Talk to someone
Icy pole: Popsicle
Jumper: Sweater

Lemon squash: Lemonade
Lollies: Sweets
Lolly water: Soda
Ring, tingle: Call someone
Sheila: Woman
Tucker: Food
Yabber: Talk

Eating in Oz

Australia's diversity is represented in the international foods enjoyed there. But the country also has plenty of uniquely Australian cuisine, including smoked emu, John Dory fillets, Balmain bugs, damper biscuits, barramundi, and kangaroo! Emu is also eaten as a pizza topping.

Vegemite is an iconic Australian food. A vegemite sandwich is as common as a peanut butter and jelly in America.

Witchetty grubs, or ghost moth larvae, have been a **staple** of the Aboriginal diet for centuries. They are dug from the trunks and roots of gum trees in the summer.

witchetty grub

Balmain bug

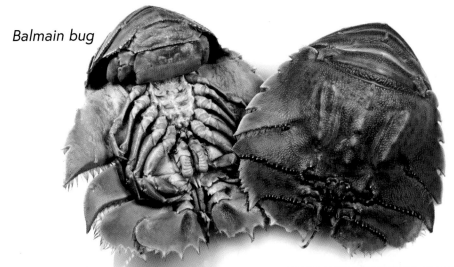

John Dory fish fillet

grilled barramundi

Aussie Sights

Many of Australia's landmarks are famous worldwide. Some are manmade, others are natural.

Sydney Opera House is a World Heritage Site. It's been called a masterpiece of human creativity for its architectural form and structural design.

The Sydney Harbour Bridge is the world's biggest steel bridge and one of Australia's most iconic landmarks. Locals affectionately call it "the Coathanger."

The Sydney Opera House is located at the tip of a peninsula that projects into Sydney Harbour. The building opened in 1973.

Uluru, or Ayers Rock, is an ancient sandstone **monolith** that rises more than 2,821 feet (860 meters) above sea level. That's nearly three times as high as the Eiffel Tower! It began forming about 550 million years ago. It is sacred to indigenous Australians.

The Twelve Apostles are limestone pillars that used to be connected to mainland cliffs. They were whittled by waves and wind into 150-foot (46-meter) columns.

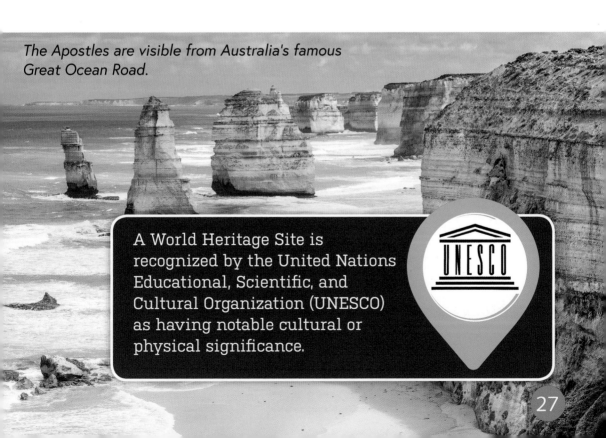

The Apostles are visible from Australia's famous Great Ocean Road.

A World Heritage Site is recognized by the United Nations Educational, Scientific, and Cultural Organization (UNESCO) as having notable cultural or physical significance.

UNESCO

Recipe: Damper Biscuits

Ingredients:

2½ cups (300 grams) plain flour

5 teaspoons (20 grams) baking powder

1 teaspoon (6 grams) salt

1 teaspoon (5 grams) butter

1 teaspoon (4 grams) sugar

1 cup (240 milliliters) milk

Directions:

1. Preheat oven to 350 degrees Fahrenheit (177 degrees Celsius).
2. Mix dry ingredients in a bowl.
3. Add butter and milk. Stir to form a dough.
4. Shape into a flattened ball and place on a greased cookie sheet.
5. Bake for 30 minutes.
6. Cut into thick slices and serve warm with butter, jam, syrup, or Vegemite!

Activity: Dot Art

Aboriginal people are known for their dot art. You can make dot art, too!

Supplies:

- Toothpicks
- Small marshmallows
- Q-tips
- Clothespins
- Cotton balls
- Paper
- Paint (various colors)
- Paper plate

Directions:

1. Insert a toothpick into a marshmallow without allowing it to go all the way through. Make at least one for each color of paint you will use.

2. Clip a clothespin to a cotton ball. Make at least one for each color of paint.

3. Pour some of each color of paint on a paper plate. Keep colors separate.

4. Using your marshmallows, cotton balls, and Q-tips, create a dot painting. You can start by drawing a figure or design on the paper and filling it in, or just paint with different size dots.

Glossary

colonizers (KAH-luh-nize-urs): people who establish a new colony or colonies in a place

federal (FED-ur-uhl): in a country with a federal government, states are united under a central authority, with states retaining state government and authority to make state laws

immigration (im-i-GRAY-shuhn): travel into a country to become a permanent resident there

indigenous (in-DIDGE-uh-nuhs): native, or originating or occurring naturally in a particular place

lingo (LEEN-goh): vocabulary or jargon of a person or group of people

monolith (MAH-nuh-lith): a large individual upright block of stone

penal (PEE-nahl): of, relating to, or involving punishment, penalties, or punitive institutions

staple (STAY-puhl): a food or product that is used regularly

teems (teems): very full of people or animals

vast (vast): very large in extent or amount

Index

Show What You Know

1. How long ago did the Aboriginals and Torres Strait Islanders arrive in Australia?
2. Who claimed Australia as a British territory?
3. Why is Australia's population so diverse?
4. Does Australia have an official language?
5. Why does Australia have so many animals that aren't found anywhere else on Earth?

Further Reading

Colson, Mary, *Indigenous Australian Cultures*, Heinemann, 2014.

Droulias, Angie and Leon, Shiela, *Kids' Travel Guide: Australia*, FlyingKids, 2017.

Kelly, Mina, *Amazing Pictures and Facts About Australia: The Most Amazing Fact Book for Kids About Australia*, CreateSpace, 2016.

About the Author

Reese Everett is an avid reader, researcher, and writer. She enjoys writing for young people because they are enthusiastic learners. Reese writes about people, places, and things she wants to learn more about. When she's not working on a book, you can find her at the beach or browsing in a bookstore.

Meet The Author!
www.meetREMauthors.com

www.rourkeeducationalmedia.com

PHOTO CREDITS: Cover & Title Pg ©4FR, ©cloki, ©Grafner, ©JonghyunKim, ©davidf, ©STRINGERimage, Top Pg Bar ©fergregory, Pg 4 ©Bardocz Peter, Pg 5 ©Albert Pego, ©kwest, ©Benny Marty, ©FiledIMAGE, Pg 6 ©Greg Brave, Pg 7 ©Rob D - Photography, ©Steffen Bollmann, Pg 8 ©Jason Benz Bennee, Pg 9 ©feelplus, ©hddigital, Pg 10 ©CrackingShots Photography, ©David Bostock, ©K.A.Willis, Pg 11 ©Robert Keresztes, ©shelley kirby, ©Anak Surasarang, ©Matt Cornish, Pg 12 ©Alberto Zornetta, ©Alizada Studios, ©worldswildlifewonders, ©totajla, Pg 13 ©Kevin Wells Photography, ©Groenewegphotography, ©Paul Looyen, ©Robyn Butler, ©Picsoftheday, Pg 14 ©Meister Photos, ©Kristian Bell, Pg 15 ©TIMICAM, ©lucky vectorstudio, Pg 16 ©superjoseph, ©AshtonEa, ©Vladimir Wrangel, Pg 17 ©Pete Niesen, ©Vlad61, ©melissaf84, Pg 18 ©ChameleonsEye, Pg 19 ©evantravels, ©David Steele, Pg 20 ©Javen, Pg 21©Fon Hodes, Pg 22 ©gary yim, Pg 23 ©Rawpixel.com, Pg 24 ©Lipowski Milan, ©jabiru, Pg 25 ©ribeiroantonio, ©Visionsi, Pg 26 ©Dan Breckwoldt, Pg 27 ©ricochet64, ©Greg Brave, Pg 28 ©bluewren, Pg 29 ©panuwat panyacharoen

Edited by: Keli Sipperley
Cover by: Rhea Magaro-Wallace
Interior design by: Corey Mills

Library of Congress PCN Data

Australia / Reese Everett
(Earth's Continents)
ISBN 978-1-64156-412-0 (hard cover)
ISBN 978-1-64156-538-7 (soft cover)
ISBN 978-1-64156-662-9 (e-Book)
Library of Congress Control Number: 2018930433

Rourke Educational Media
Printed in the United States of America,
North Mankato, Minnesota